HAL LEONARD PIANO REPERTOIRE
Book 3 • Early Intermediate

JOURNEY THROUGH THE
CLASSICS

COMPILED AND EDITED BY JENNIFER LINN

Journey Through the Classics is a four-volume piano repertoire series designed
to lead students seamlessly from the easiest classics to the intermediate masterworks.
The graded pieces are presented in a progressive order and feature a variety of classical
favorites essential to any piano student's educational foundation. The authentic
repertoire is ideal for auditions and recitals and each book includes a handy reference
chart with the key, composer, stylistic period, and challenge elements
listed for each piece.

-Jennifer Linn

Dedicated in loving memory to my mother and first teacher,
Geraldine Ruth Ryan Lange.

ISBN 978-4584-1151-8

7777 W. BLUEMOUND RD. P.O. BOX 13819 MILWAUKEE, WI 53213

In Australia Contact:
Hal Leonard Australia Pty. Ltd.
4 Lentara Court
Cheltenham, Victoria, 3192 Australia
Email: ausadmin@halleonard.com.au

Visit Hal Leonard Online at
www.halleonard.com

JOURNEY THROUGH THE CLASSICS:
Book 3 Reference Chart

✔ WHEN COMPLETED	PAGE	TITLE	COMPOSER	ERA	KEY	METER	CHALLENGE ELEMENTS
	5	Etude	Czerny	Classical	C	$\frac{4}{4}$	Both hands in 𝄞; repeated notes in LH; legato harmonic intervals
	6	Arabesque	Burgmüller	Romantic	Am	$\frac{2}{4}$	16th notes; RH and LH shifts; legato/staccato coordination
	8	Humming Song	Schumann	Romantic	C	$\frac{3}{4}$	Both hands in 𝄞; legato touch; balance and melody/accompaniment in one hand
	10	Russian Folk Song	Beethoven	Classical	Am	$\frac{2}{4}$	Vertical reading; shifting chords
	11	The Bear	Rebikoff	Romantic	C	$\frac{2}{4}$	Both hands in 𝄢; broken LH octaves; reading accidentals
	12	Musette	Bach (notebook)	Baroque	D	$\frac{2}{4}$	D major key signature; 16th notes; quick hand shifts; legato/staccato coordination
	14	Sonatina in G	Attwood	Classical	G	$\frac{4}{4}$	Alberti bass; legato/staccato coordination; articulation and phrasing
	16	Ecossaise	Beethoven	Classical	G	$\frac{2}{4}$	Broken LH octave shifts; 16th notes; syncopation; D.C. al Fine
	17	Tarantella	Spindler	Romantic	C	$\frac{3}{8}$	$\frac{3}{8}$ time signature; very fast scale passages; legato/staccato coordination
	20	Russian Polka	Glinka	Romantic	Dm	$\frac{2}{4}$	16th notes; frequent LH shifts; accents; legato/staccato coordination
	21	Spanish Dance	Oesten	Romantic	Am	$\frac{3}{4}$	16th notes; repeating LH chords; accents; articulation
	22	Sonatina in C	Latour	Classical	C	$\frac{4}{4}$	Continuous scale patterns; LH/RH coordination
	24	Wild Rider	Schumann	Romantic	Am	$\frac{6}{8}$	Fingerings in broken chord patterns; staccato touch; frequent hand shifts
	26	Theme and Variation	Gurlitt	Romantic	G	$\frac{2}{4}$	Connecting pedal; portato touch; phrasing; triplets; balance
	28	Sonatina in C	Clementi	Classical	C	𝄵	Scale passages; alberti bass; broken arpeggios in both hands; articulation
	30	Minuet and Trio	Mozart, W.A.	Classical	G	$\frac{3}{4}$	Articulation and phrasing; triplets; 16th notes; frequent hand shifts
	32	Menuet in D Minor	Bach (notebook)	Baroque	Dm	$\frac{3}{4}$	Contrapuntal style; frequent hand shifts; leaping intervals; LH/RH coordination
	34	Solfeggio	Bach, J.C.F.	Baroque	D	𝄵	Continuous 16th note passages; fingerings in broken chord patterns
	36	Minuet in G	Bach (notebook)	Baroque	G	$\frac{3}{4}$	Broken chord arpeggios in both hands; triplets; articulation
	38	Tolling Bell	Heller	Romantic	Bm	$\frac{3}{4}$	Pedal technique; broken chord patterns in both hands; choreography of both hands
	40	Bourrée in E Minor	Bach, J.S.	Baroque	Em	𝄵	Articulation and phrasing; LH/RH coordination; frequent hand shifts
	42	The Limpid Stream	Burgmüller	Romantic	G	$\frac{4}{4}$	Balance with melody/accompaniment in one hand; LH melody; triplets
	44	The Murmuring Brook	Gurlitt	Romantic	G	$\frac{2}{4}$	Balance with melody/accompaniment in one hand; LH melody; 16th notes
	46	Quiet Morning	Maykapar	Romantic	F	$\frac{12}{8}$	Pedal technique; $\frac{12}{8}$ time signature; balance and beauty of tone
	47	Waltz	Schubert	Romantic	B♭	$\frac{3}{4}$	Vertical reading, B-flat key signature; balance between hands, articulation

CONTENTS

Etude
Op. 823, No. 2

Carl Czerny
(1791-1857)

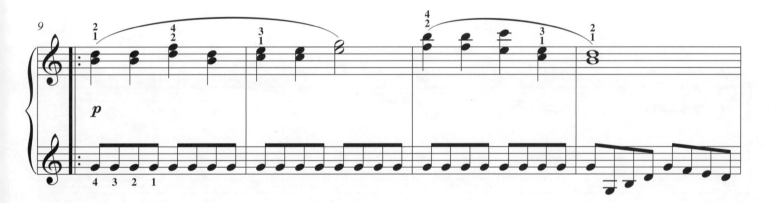

Arabesque
Op. 100, No. 2

Friedrich Burgmüller
(1806-1874)

Allegro scherzando

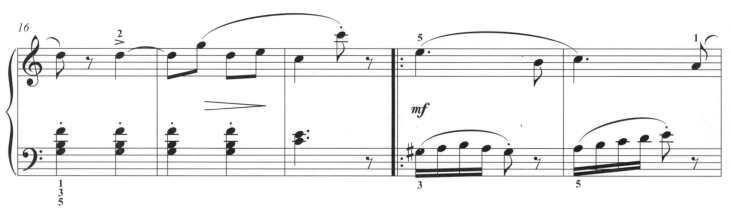

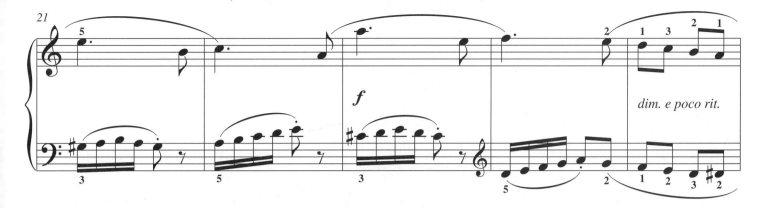

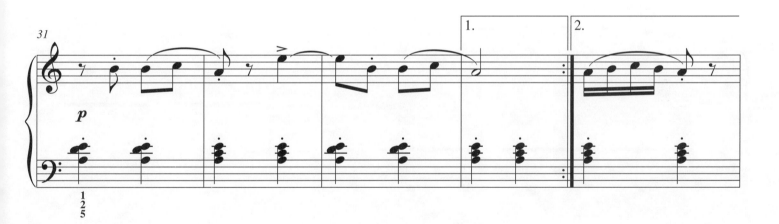

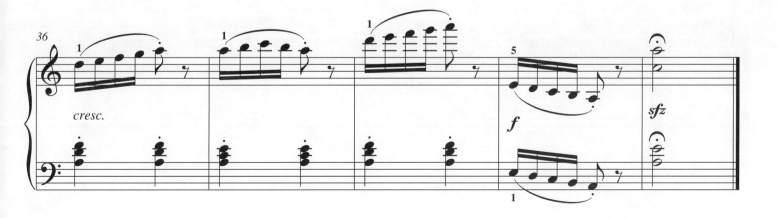

Humming Song
Op. 68, No. 3

Robert Schumann
(1810-1856)

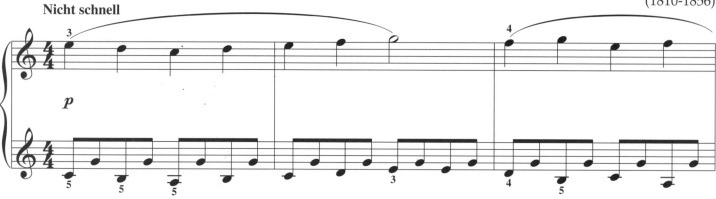

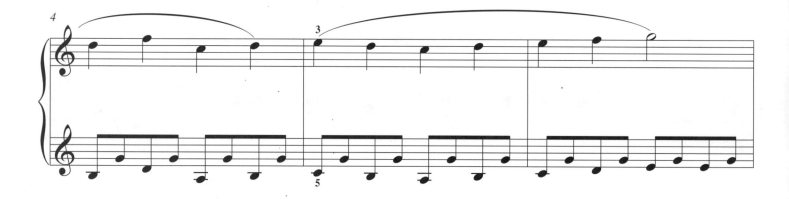

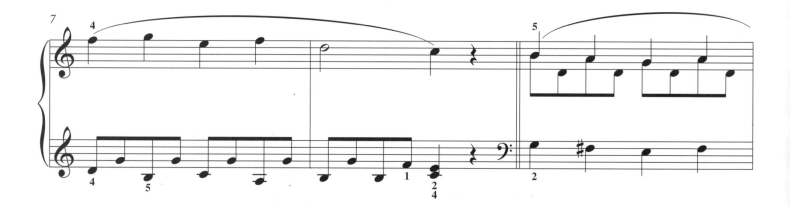

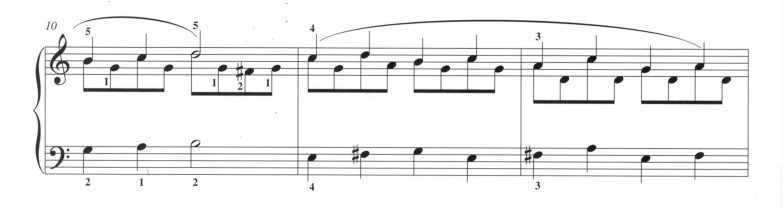

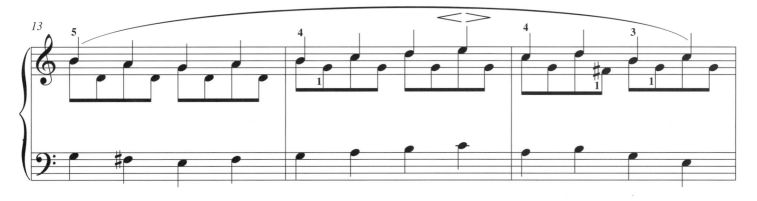

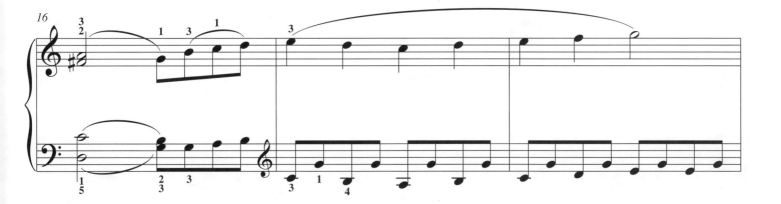

Russian Folk Song

Op. 107, No. 7

Ludwig van Beethoven
(1770-1827)

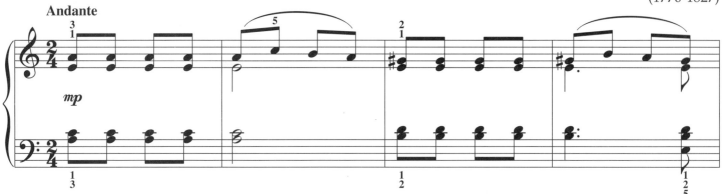

The Bear

Vladimir Rebikoff
(1866-1920)

Andante pesante

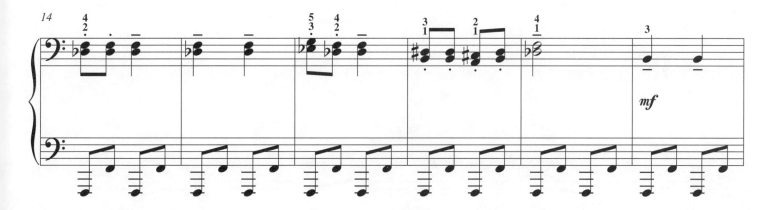

Musette

Notebook for Anna Magdalena Bach
18th century

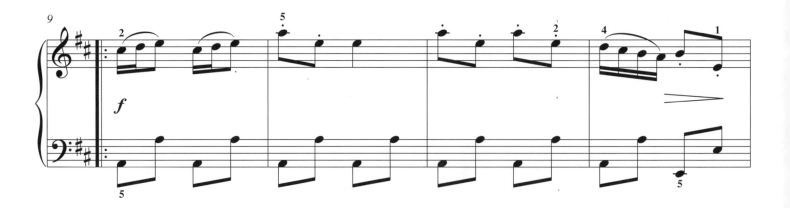

Sonatina in G

Thomas Attwood
(1765-1838)

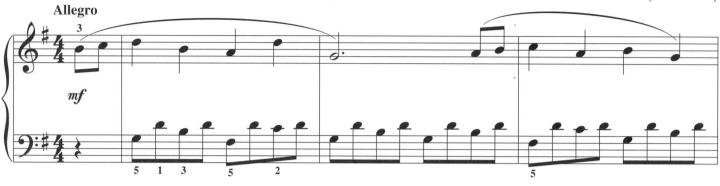

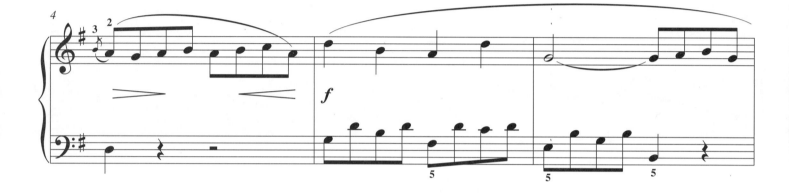

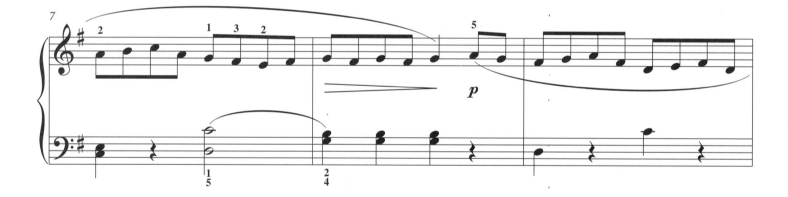

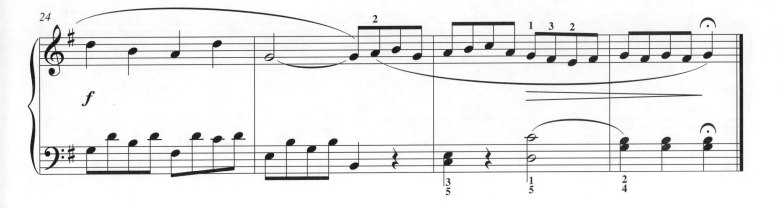

Ecossaise

Ludwig van Beethoven
(1770-1827)

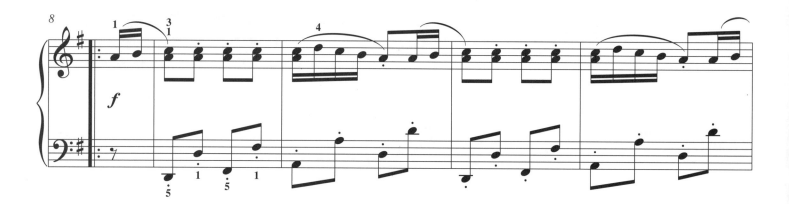

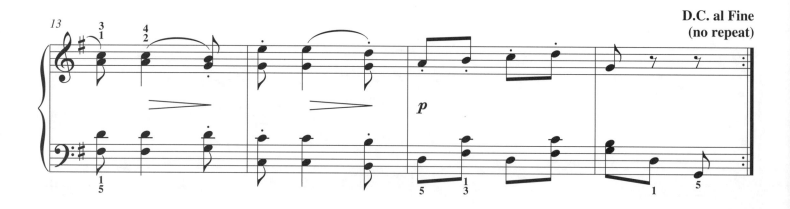

Tarantella
Op. 157, No. 1

Fritz Spindler
(1817-1905)

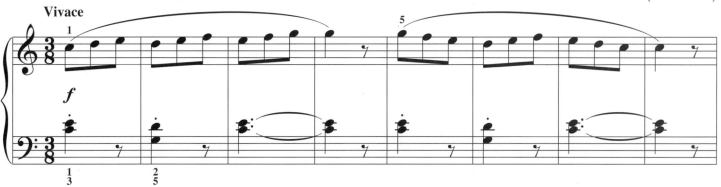

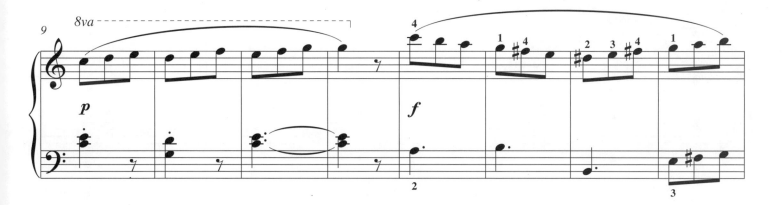

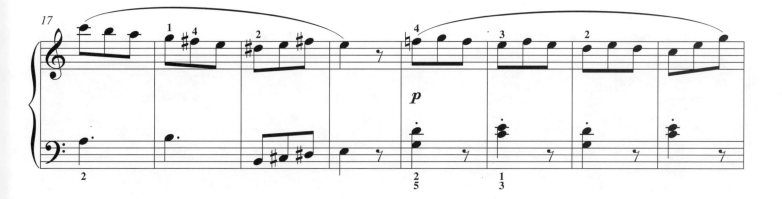

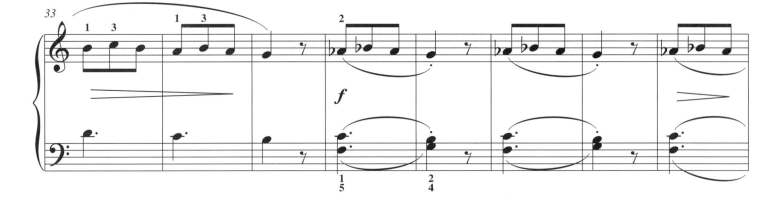

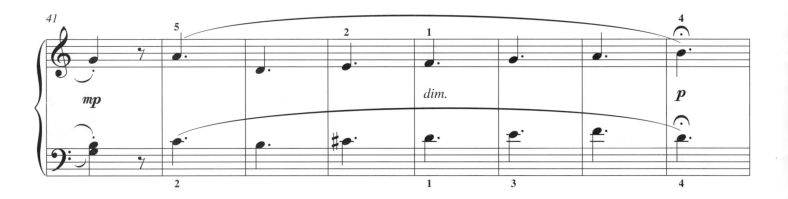

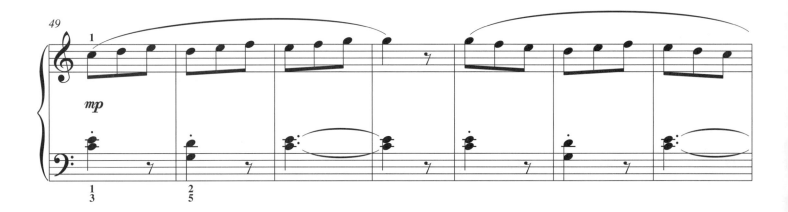

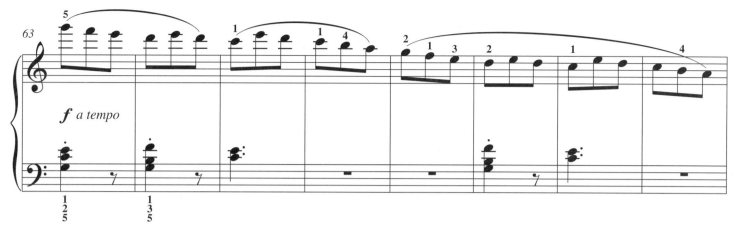

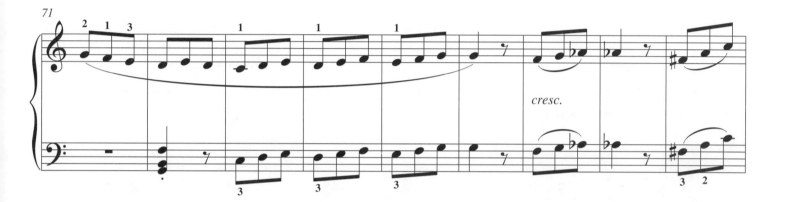

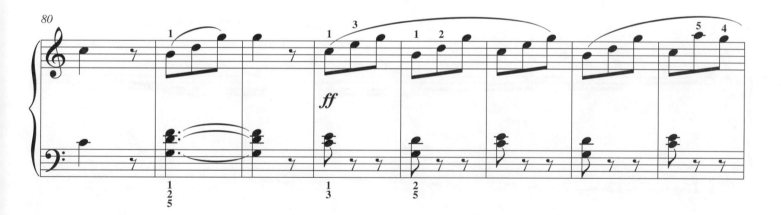

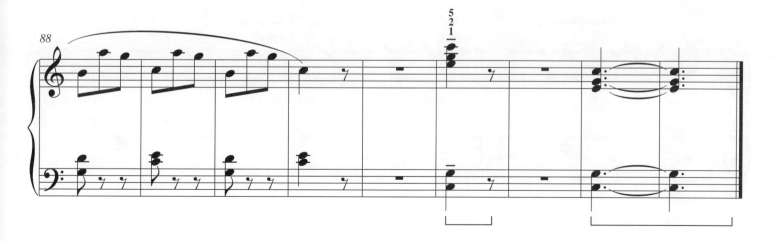

Russian Polka

Michael Ivanovich Glinka
(1804-1857)

Spanish Dance
Op. 61, No. 10

Theodor Oesten
(1813-1870)

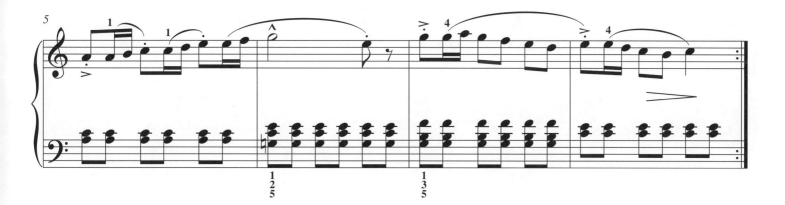

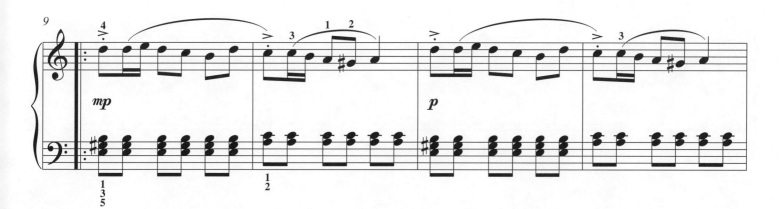

Sonatina in C

Jean T. Latour
(1766-1837)

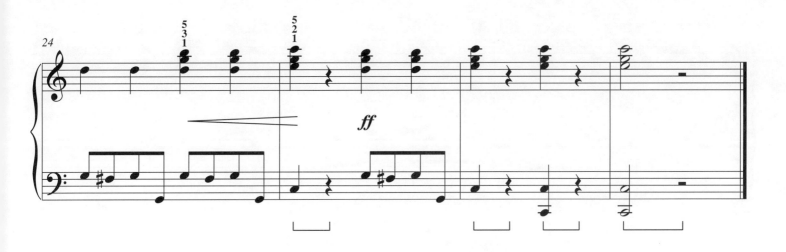

Wild Rider
Op. 68, No. 8

Robert Schumann
(1810-1856)

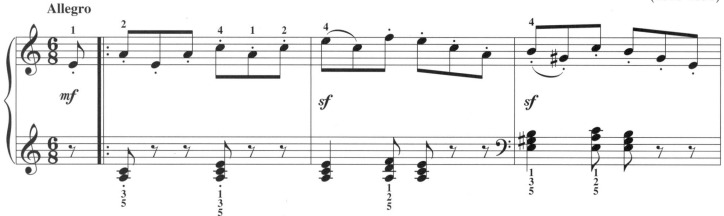

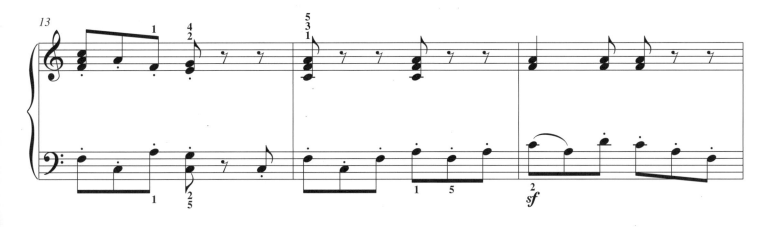

Theme and Variation
Op. 228

Cornelius Gurlitt
(1820-1901)

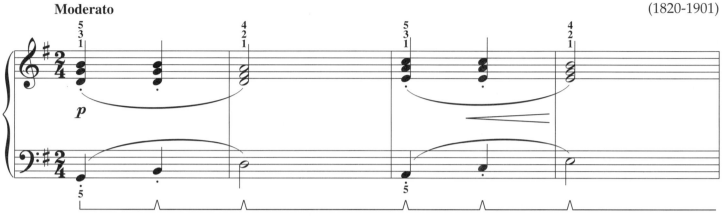

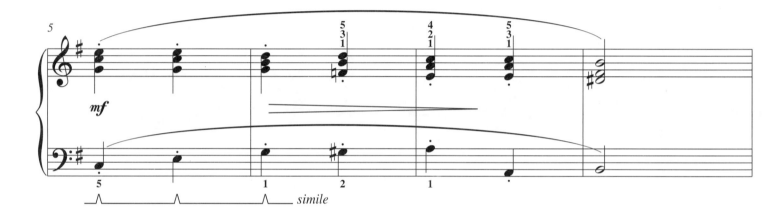

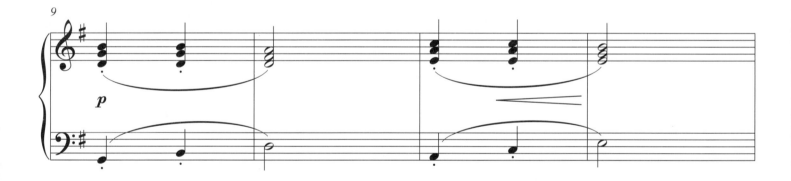

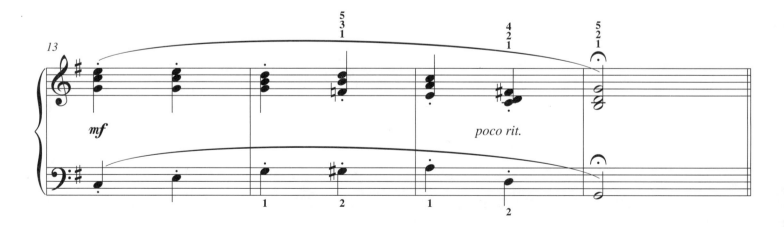

VARIATION

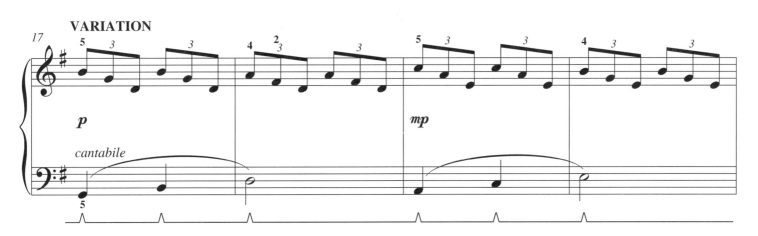

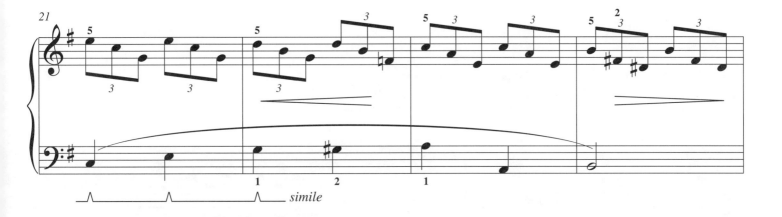

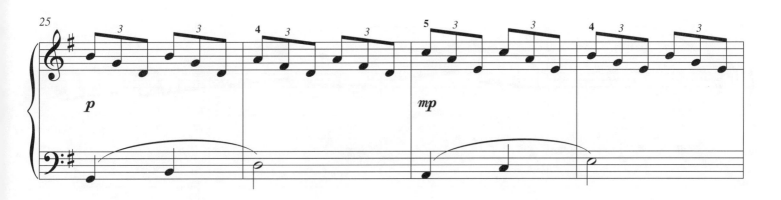

Sonatina in C

I

Muzio Clementi
(1752-1832)

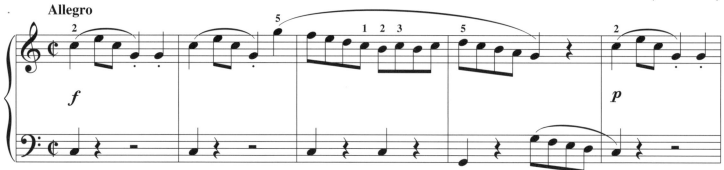

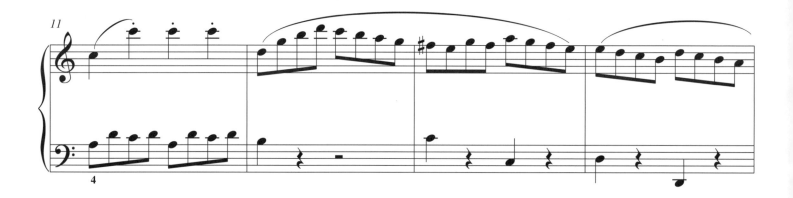

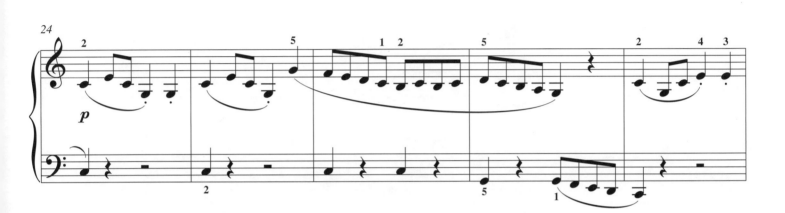

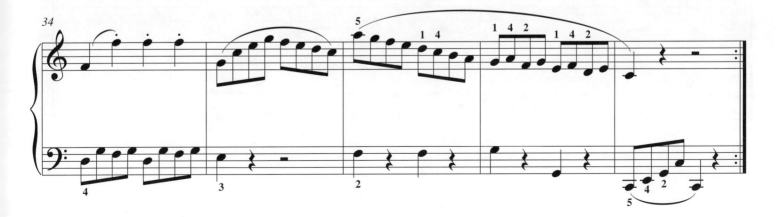

Minuet and Trio

Wolfgang Amadeus Mozart
(1756-1791)

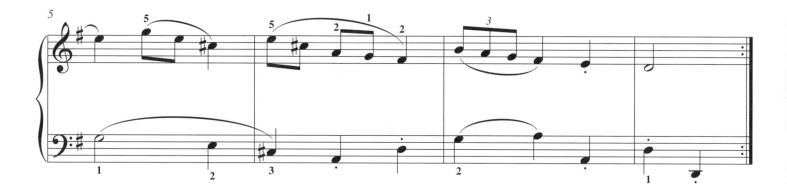

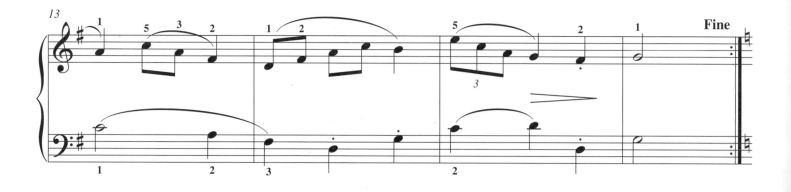

Trio

D.C. al Fine
2nd time

Menuet in D Minor

Notebook for Anna Magdalena Bach
18th century

Solfeggio

Johann Christoph Friedrich Bach
(1732-1795)

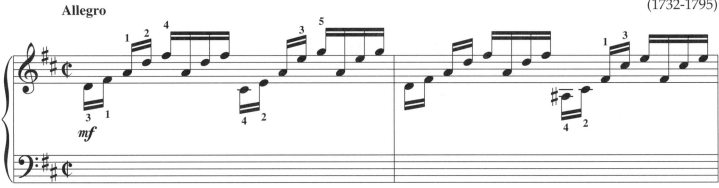

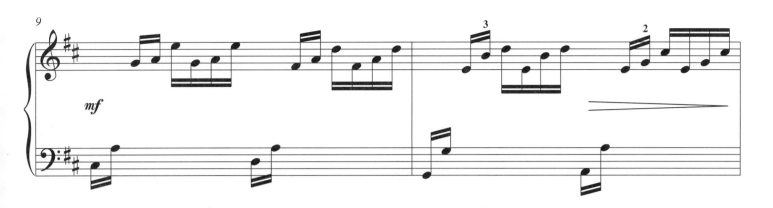

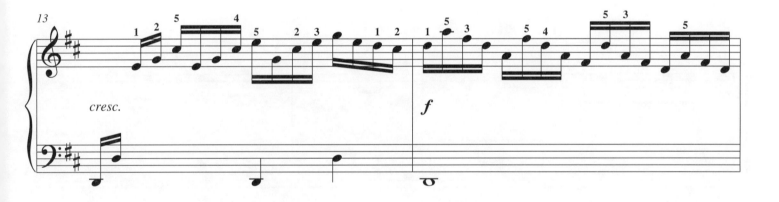

Minuet in G

Notebook for Anna Magdalena Bach
18th century

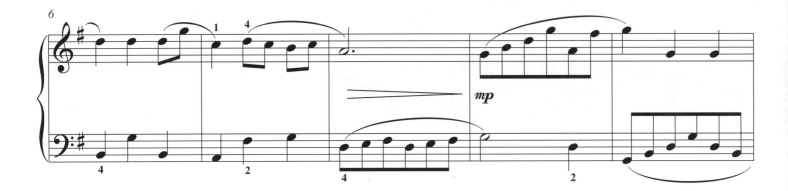

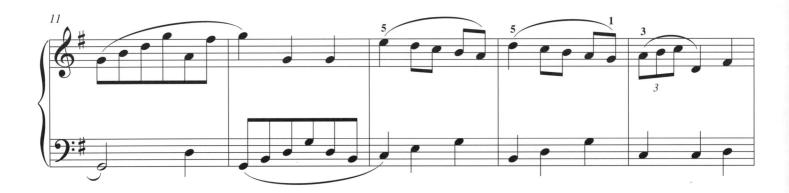

Tolling Bell

Op. 125, No. 8

Stephen Heller
(1813-1888)

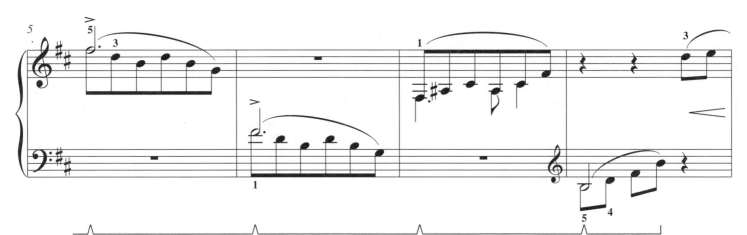

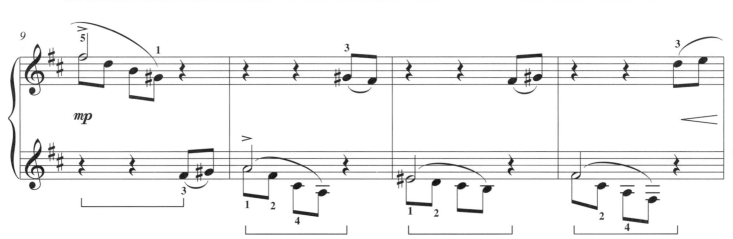

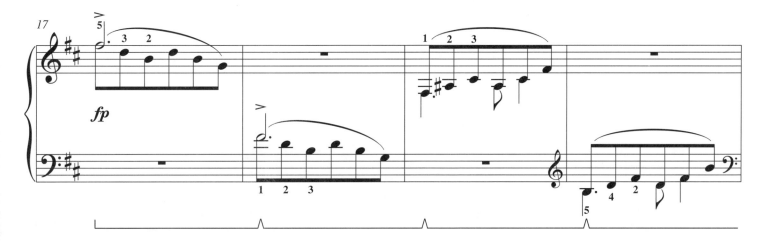

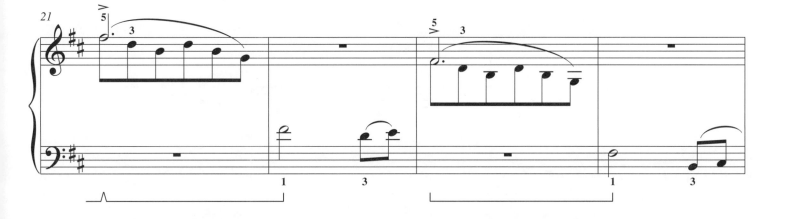

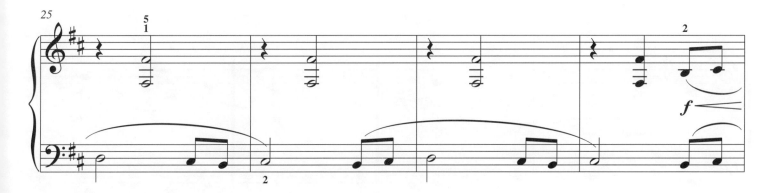

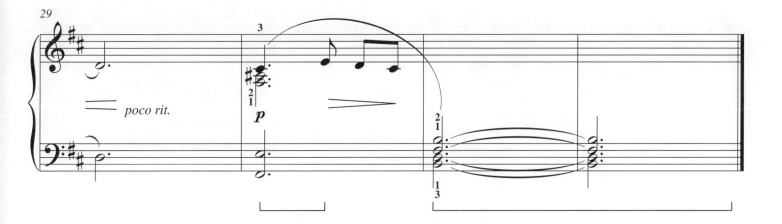

Bourrée in E Minor
BWV 996

Johann Sebastian Bach
(1685-1750)

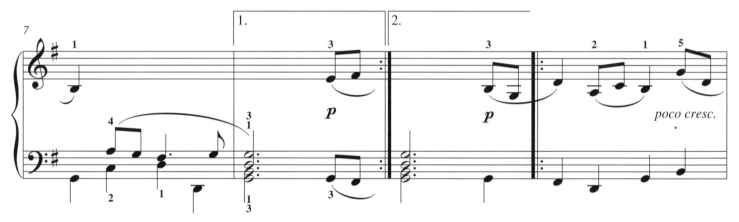

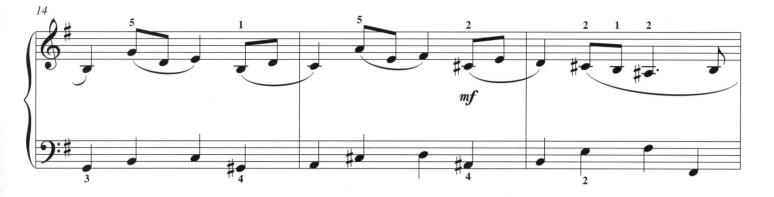

The Limpid Stream

Op. 100, No. 7

Friedrich Burgmüller
(1806-1874)

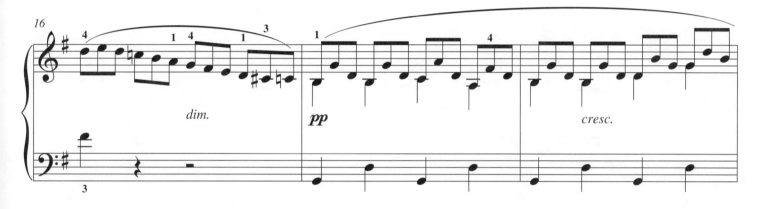

The Murmuring Brook
Op. 140, No. 5

Cornelius Gurlitt
(1820-1901)

Quiet Morning

Samuel Maykapar
(1867-1938)

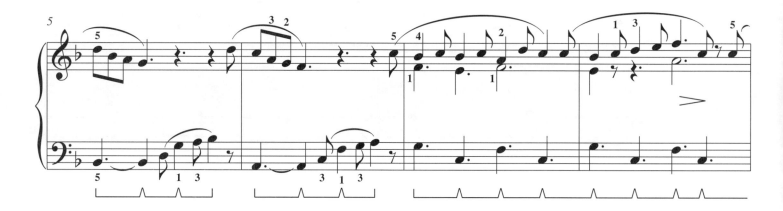

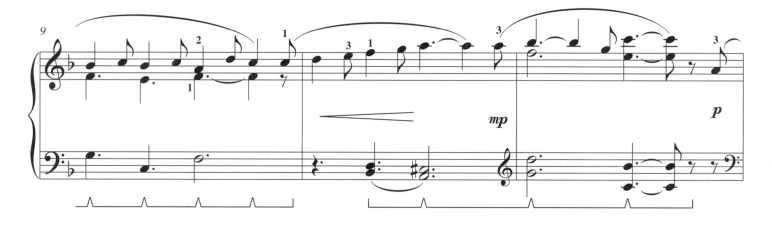

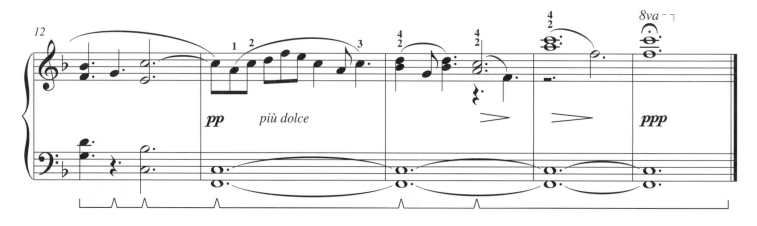

Waltz
Op. 127, No. 15

Franz Schubert
(1797-1828)

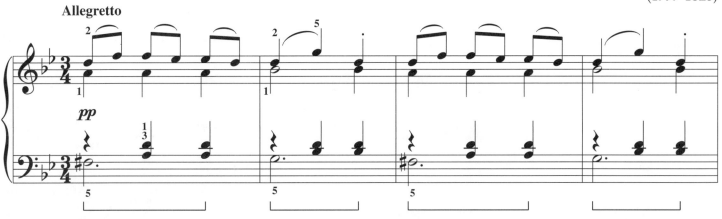